TEENS HELPING TEENS

Making a Difference

Leanne Currie-McGhee

ReferencePoint Press

San Diego, CA

Printed in the United States

For more information, contact:
ReferencePoint Press, Inc.
PO Box 27779
San Diego, CA 92198
www.ReferencePointPress.com

LIBRARY OF CONGRESS CATALOGING-IN-PUBLICATION DATA

Names: Currie-McGhee, Leanne, 1971- author.
Title: Teens helping teens : making a difference / by Leanne Currie-McGhee.
Description: San Diego, CA : ReferencePoint Press, Inc., 2026. | Includes bibliographical references and index. | Audience term: Teenagers
Identifiers: LCCN 2024053798 (print) | LCCN 2024053799 (ebook) | ISBN 9781678212063 (library binding) | ISBN 9781678212070 (ebook)
Subjects: LCSH: Teenagers--Social conditions--Juvenile literature. | Teenagers--Life skills guides--Juvenile literature. | Adolescent psychology--Juvenile literature.
Classification: LCC HQ796 .C8985 2026 (print) | LCC HQ796 (ebook) | DDC 305.235--dc23/eng/20250108
LC record available at https://lccn.loc.gov/2024053798
LC ebook record available at https://lccn.loc.gov/2024053799

CONTENTS

Introduction 4
Teens Can Have an Impact

Chapter One 8
Many Needs, Many Benefits

Chapter Two 17
Teens Supporting Bullied Peers

Chapter Three 27
Teens Tutoring Teens

Chapter Four 36
Teen Mentors

Chapter Five 44
Mental Health Help

Source Notes 53
For Further Research 56
Index 59
Picture Credits 63
About the Author 64

Teens Can Have an Impact

Sometimes being a teen can feel overwhelming. Between school pressures, social challenges, and the emotional roller coaster of growing up, it is common for teens to face struggles. Vaishnavi Kumbala experienced these pressures in high school, particularly during the COVID-19 pandemic, when many schools shifted to online learning. "Stress levels were running high, so I wanted to do something to help people manage their stress,"[1] Kumbala shared in an interview. She knew something needed to change but did not want to wait for someone else to step in.

In 2021 Kumbala created an app called Saplings. Her app provides teens with ways to manage stress and improve mental well-being. It does this with guided exercises, relaxation techniques, a journal, and links to mental health resources. It also includes a peer support feature, allowing users to connect with each other so that they can offer encouragement, advice, or just a friendly ear.

Seeing a Need

Kumbala designed her app the way she did because she believes that teens are uniquely able to help other teens. She knew she did not need to be an adult or professional to find a way to help her peers. She believes that the most effective support often comes from those who understand what others are going through because they have had similar experiences. These experiences might involve stress from academics, social issues, bullying, or mental health concerns. Whatever the source of the problem, shared experiences make teens uniquely positioned to notice a problem affecting a peer—and act on it.

> "Stress levels were running high, so I wanted to do something to help people manage their stress."[1]
>
> —Vaishnavi Kumbala, teen who created a mental health app for teens

In Kumbala's case, her app started as a local project and now is impacting teens across the country. "I wanted to do something that merged health care with technology to help more people," she says. "It makes me feel really good that something I created is able to help even just one person."[2] Since its release, her app has been downloaded by thousands of teens nationwide. Becky Stutzman, a mental health coordinator for Lincoln Parish Public Schools in Louisiana, shared Kumbala's app with mental health counselors in her district and promoted its use. Then in 2021 Kumbala's app won first place in the Congressional App Challenge in Washington, DC, and was showcased in the US Capitol building.

Why Teens Can Impact Others

What also makes teens particularly effective at helping their peers is that they see them regularly. They are often the first ones to notice when a friend is feeling down, distressed, unhappy, or left out. This was the case for Matthew Certner, a high school student in New Jersey. Certner became concerned about a family friend who really liked playing sports but could not connect with a league or team that fit his needs. Certner's friend had been diagnosed with autism, and Certner suspected he was being left out because of this. Certner said that he and his brother both "saw that our friend really wasn't being included [in athletics] when it came to recreational leagues or even just at school."[3] He realized that he had access to athletic programs that his friend did not have. So Certner and his brother got together with friends and classmates who often played basketball. They created a free weekly clinic where kids and teens with disabilities could participate in athletic activities with

Teens are particularly effective at helping their peers because they see each other regularly. They are often the first ones to notice when a friend is feeling down, distressed, unhappy, or left out.

Certner and his friends. Eventually, this led to the formation of Certner's nonprofit organization, the Special Needs Athletic Program.

The clinic became a major success. Eventually, the mother of one of the participants took over the program, with teens and young adults on the board to ensure its continuation. Since then, the program has expanded throughout New Jersey and beyond, offering sports sessions, activities, and educational events. Today volunteers aged twelve to twenty-two coach and mentor participants, who range in age from five to eighteen. It all goes back to Certner and his brother seeing a need. "I was always big with sports. So was my brother. And seeing someone that we knew not being included . . . when it comes to sports, we knew we could do something. And we did,"[4] Certner recalls.

Own Experience

Experiencing hardship is another powerful motivation for teens to help other teens. Often, teens who have overcome obstacles are motivated to make sure others do not go through those experiences without support. Kristina Saffran and Liana Rosenman were two teens who took this idea to heart. After battling anorexia during their teenage years and meeting at an eating disorder treatment center, they realized that recovery resources were limited for many. Many young people suffering from an eating disorder do not have the financial means to pay for help. Instead of letting that discourage them, Saffran and Rosenman took action. Together, they cofounded Project HEAL to help provide support and treatment for teens dealing with eating disorders.

The two wanted to ensure that youth had access to different types of treatment resources and could connect with others as they worked to overcome their eating disorders. Their work has allowed teens across the nation to access help. Over the past fifteen years, Project HEAL has grown from a small initiative to a nationwide organization. It has provided treatment scholarships, peer mentorship, and advocacy for eating disorder awareness, helping countless teens on their recovery journey.

The Impact of Helping

Teens who work to support their peers also experience their own growth. Helping other people builds empathy, strengthens communication skills, and can boost self-esteem. When teens help others, they gain valuable life experience that will serve them well into adulthood. For many, it also sets them on a lifelong path of helping others. As Kumbala put it, "It has been really fulfilling to help other people, and it's been a fantastic journey so far, but I still have a long way to go."[5]

Whether it's organizing support groups, volunteering time, or simply offering a listening ear, peer support is one of the most powerful tools for overcoming the challenges of the teenage years. While there are times that teens may need professional help, such as getting therapy or seeing a doctor, often peer help is a part of the solution to their struggles. What many teens have realized is that making an impact is not about how old you are but how willing you are to act. By helping others, teens not only change lives but also create a ripple effect of kindness and support that benefits everyone involved.

Many Needs, Many Benefits

Christopher Gonzalez, now a young adult, distinctly remembers feeling anxious and alone while in high school. During his freshman year his parents were going through a divorce, and Gonzalez struggled with his emotions. Then he heard that his school offered peer counseling. The idea of talking to someone his own age seemed less intimidating than talking to an adult. Going through the counseling improved his mental health and ability to handle the divorce.

The following year, Gonzalez decided that he wanted to help other students the way he had been helped. So he decided to become a peer counselor. He enjoyed it so much that he continued in this role all through high school. What Gonzalez realized, after receiving help and giving help, is that many teens just need someone to listen and show understanding. This is what he did with a classmate who talked about being in a gang, drinking too much, and feeling depressed. As a peer counselor, Gonzalez listened carefully, talked with the classmate on multiple occasions, and also shared that he too had experienced feelings of depression. In conversations with Gonzalez, the classmate realized he was not alone. This helped him get to a point of feeling better about himself and his life—similar to what Gonzalez experienced during his own sessions with a peer counselor. "Without peer counseling," Gonzalez says, "I don't know where I'd be. . . . If there was peer counseling in every high school in the country, I feel we'd have fewer kids who are depressed, and I think we'd be in a much better place overall."[6]

Like Gonzales, many teens feel overwhelmed by events taking place in their lives. From navigating academic pressures to dealing with mental health concerns, teens often find themselves at a crossroads, unsure of where to turn. However, there's a powerful resource at their disposal: their peers. Teens helping other teens can be life changing, providing a type of support that adults sometimes cannot. And when teens help others, they gain self-confidence, empathy, and a stronger connection to their peers.

Many Challenges

Teens today face a variety of challenges, many of which can negatively affect their emotional well-being. Family financial struggles, abuse, bullying, academic pressures, confusion over gender identity, worries about body image, and the constant presence of social

Many teens feel overwhelmed by events taking place in their lives. From navigating academic pressures to dealing with mental health concerns, they often find themselves unsure of where to turn.

media are among the issues encountered by teens. These issues can lead to feelings of isolation, anxiety, and an overwhelming sense of unease. For many teens, it becomes difficult to navigate these pressures alone, which is why peer support is so critical.

Anxiety and depression are among the most pressing problems teens face. According to the National Institute of Mental Health, about 14.7 percent of US adolescents aged twelve to seventeen experienced at least one major depressive episode in 2021. Depression often presents itself as persistent feelings of hopelessness, hindering a teen's ability to engage in everyday activities like school or social interactions. "I just completely stopped doing all the things I enjoyed doing. Even if I tried to get out of bed to do any hobbies or see friends, my body physically wouldn't let me out of bed,"[7] explains Chrissy, a teen recovering from depression. Retreating from life's daily activities increases isolation, leading to even greater feelings of loneliness.

Bullying is another widespread problem for teens. The Bureau of Justice Statistics and the National Center for Education Statistics reported that 19 percent of twelve- to eighteen-year-old students were bullied at school from 2021 to 2022. Bullying can lead to a range of emotional problems, including low self-esteem, anxiety, and in severe cases, thoughts of suicide. Those who are bullied often find it hard to reach out for help from adults, which is why peer support networks are essential.

Social media, while offering a way for teens to connect with friends, also presents its own set of challenges. A 2022 survey conducted by the Pew Research Center found that 38 percent of teens say they feel overwhelmed by all the drama they see on social media, 30 percent say social media has made them feel like their friends are leaving them out of things, and 23 percent say these platforms make them feel worse about their own lives. For many teens, social media can amplify their insecurities and lead them to constantly compare themselves to others.

The issues facing teens can create a cycle of stress and isolation that many find hard to escape. This is why peers can be an ef-

Teens Mobilizing for Social Change

In 2019 a group of high school students in Parkland, Florida, inspired by their tragic experiences of gun violence at their school, launched a movement called March for Our Lives. This grassroots organization was founded after the tragic mass shooting at Marjory Stoneman Douglas High School and aimed to advocate for stronger gun control measures. The teens organized a national march that drew hundreds of thousands of participants in Washington, DC, and cities across the country, sending a powerful message about the need for change to help their peers. Their efforts raised awareness about gun violence and its effect on teens and empowered other teens to engage in political activism for change in their lives. Through their advocacy, these teens have used their voices to inspire change in policies and actions that affect them and their peers.

fective source of help. When teens support each other—whether by listening, sharing experiences, or offering advice—they provide a sense of understanding. Peer-to-peer support offers teens a safe space to share their experiences, connect with others facing similar struggles, and ultimately feel less alone.

Why Teens Can Help

Teens are uniquely positioned to help each other because they share many of the same experiences and challenges, allowing for a deep level of empathy and understanding. Knowing this, many teens feel more comfortable confiding in a peer. This makes peer support an essential resource in schools and social groups. Additionally, teens are often more open and candid with their peers than they are with adults. A 2021 C.S. Mott Children's Hospital National Poll on Children's Health found that three-quarters of parents of teens felt that peer support leaders would better understand struggles of teens, compared to teachers or school counselors. For this reason, in 2022 freshman Baylee McPherson trained to be a peer counselor through a program at Clovis West High School in California. "I think some students feel more comfortable talking to other students because we understand what they're going through," she said. "They think adults are just going to try to solve their problems for them or call their parents. That's a big fear."[8]

Also, teens spend most of their time around other teens, making peer support easily accessible. Whether in school, extracurricular activities, or at social events, other teens are readily available to offer help. This was true for Angeles Perez, a junior at Pomona High School in Los Angeles in 2021. It had been a challenging year for Perez. At home, her parents didn't accept her queer identity, and she was diagnosed with type 1 diabetes, which meant giving up her usual comfort foods like chips. Feeling isolated, she was unsure who to turn to. Then she heard about trained peer support counselors at her school. When she began meeting with a peer counselor, she could release her emotions without being judged. Her peer counselor mostly listened. Perez said she got what she needed—someone who would listen to her without constantly giving opinions. She had also spoken with an

Teens spend most of their time around other teens, making peer support easily accessible. Whether in school or extracurricular activities, other teens are readily available to offer help.

adult counselor but said it was easier to open up to another teen. "In peer counseling, I can talk however I want because I'm with another teenager," she said. "I know they'll get it."[9]

Benefits to Helpers

Teens who receive help from their peers are not the only ones who benefit from this interaction. Teens who give help—who provide support to peers—gain from the experience as well. One of the most significant benefits is a sense of empowerment. When teens engage in peer support, they often feel more capable and confident in their ability to make a difference in the world. For instance, youth chapters of the Black Lives Matter (BLM) movement have given teens a platform to actively combat racism and advocate for societal change to help their peers. One example of a teen involved in the BLM movement is Thandiwe Abdullah. Along with her siblings, she cocreated the BLM Youth Vanguard and helped launch the Black Lives Matter at School program. One of her major accomplishments was the successful removal of random searches from the Los Angeles Unified School District. This experience has taught her that she can make a change in her peers' lives and the world, no matter what her age. "I think my biggest goal is to help young people understand that the world we know right now is not something we have to just sit back and accept,"[10] Abdullah says.

> **"I think my biggest goal is to help young people understand that the world we know right now is not something we have to just sit back and accept."[10]**
>
> —Thandiwe Abdullah, Black Lives Matter youth activist

In addition to feeling empowered, teens supporting other teens also experience enhanced self-esteem. A study published in the *Journal of Adolescence* revealed that teens who acted as mentors reported higher levels of confidence and a stronger sense of purpose. This boost in self-esteem can have long-lasting effects, helping teens develop into more self-assured individuals who are ready to face life's challenges.

> "[Being a peer counselor] taught me beautiful communication skills and coping mechanisms. I take better care of myself."[11]
>
> —Baylee McPherson, high school peer counselor

Beyond emotional growth, teens who help other teens also acquire valuable lifetime skills. When providing peer support, teens develop communication, problem-solving, and teamwork abilities—all of which are essential for personal and professional success. Baylee McPherson discovered this when she decided to become a peer counselor. Like all prospective peer counselors, she was required to take a class that focused on how to handle friendship issues and depression, how to read tone and body language, how to ask the right questions, and how to know when to involve an adult. Then, she began meeting with one or two students a day for about thirty minutes each. In all of those sessions, she listened to their struggles and concerns with an empathetic ear. "I get way more out of it than I give," McPherson says. "It's taught me beautiful communication skills and coping mechanisms. I take better care of myself. I've developed bonds with people that won't break."[11]

Different Ways Teens Support

Teens support each other in various ways. This can include small, individual actions or large-scale initiatives. The most common way teens help is by joining established organizations that provide peer support services. A notable example is the Trevor Project, which offers crisis intervention and counseling for LGBTQ youth. A national survey conducted by the Trevor Project in 2021 found that 40 percent of LGBTQ youth had considered suicide in the past year. This finding emphasizes the critical need for providing mental health support. Youth aged eighteen and up can volunteer to become a trained volunteer crisis counselor. These volunteers provide real-time support, either by texts or phone calls, to LGBTQ youth in crisis. They provide emotional support to their peers, creating a powerful sense of community and safety.

Some young people do more than join an organization. Some create their own program based on personal experiences. At age eight, with her parents' help, Sadie Keller founded the Sadie Keller Foundation to help kids with cancer. Keller was diagnosed with acute lymphoblastic leukemia when she was seven. Over the next two and a half years, she received different treatments, including chemotherapy. She received her last treatment in 2017 and as of 2021 she was still cancer free. In the midst of her battle, at age eight, she decided to create a program to uplift the spirits of other children who were undergoing cancer treatments. Her foundation provides Christmas presents to kids who are in the hospital battling cancer and gifts when they celebrate treatment milestones such as the end of chemotherapy. Additionally, the foundation raises money for childhood cancer research. Keller explains, "I try to use my story to bring awareness to cancer and have made a foundation to help kids going through cancer and put a smile on their face."[12]

Like Keller, Jordan Somer started her own organization to support and empower other young people. Somer's focus was youth with disabilities. She grew up participating in beauty pageants and gained confidence in herself through these pageants. At age

Teen's Fundraising Effort Makes a Difference

At age fifteen, Gabriel Donovan lived with neurofibromatosis type 1, a genetic condition that can come with both physical issues such as benign tumors and learning difficulties such as attention and comprehension struggles. He met Lilly, a fourteen-year-old girl who relied on a ventilator to breathe after a car crash that also took her mother's life. The damage from the crash hindered her ability to communicate easily. Donovan discovered she needed a piece of assistive technology that would help her communicate better with people and allow her to attend high school. She could not afford the technology. Donovan decided to do something. He created a fundraising campaign using social media to spread the word. Donovan created a design featuring flowers, inspired by Lilly's name, for tote bags and T-shirts to raise funds and awareness for her needs, calling it the Adirondack Lilly. He ended up raising $50,000, which exceeded his aim of $16,000, the amount needed for Lilly's technology. For Donovan, understanding the frustrations of dealing with a disability resulted in his passion to find a way to empower Lilly.

thirteen, after volunteering at the Special Olympics, Somer wanted to give disabled girls more opportunities to gain self-esteem. She founded the Miss Amazing organization to hold pageants for girls with disabilities. In these pageants, every participant is a winner and gains a crown. Today the organization operates in more than thirty states. It still holds pageants, but it has expanded to provide leadership skills and self-advocacy programs.

Skylar Jones has taken part in several Miss Amazing pageants. Jones has developmental delays and attention-deficit/hyperactivity disorder (ADHD), and she has struggled with a lack of confidence and has difficulty making friends. She shares, "With my disability, it's hard to make friends. . . . I didn't feel like there was a community out there for me to belong to."[13] She started attending Miss Amazing at age sixteen and continued for several years. The Miss Amazing pageant is a day-long affair. On that day, each participant gets her hair and makeup done, participates in singing and dancing, and engages in shared activities of motivation, self-discovery, and friendship. Through these pageants, Jones found a sense of belonging and self-confidence, enjoying the community and personal growth the event offers.

While joining or starting an organization can be a major way to positively impact peers, so can simpler actions. Listening to a friend, offering advice, or standing up against bullying can have a profound impact on others. These more personal acts of kindness can help another teen through a difficult time. No matter how they do so, teens who take the initiative to support their peers not only create a meaningful impact on others but also experience significant personal growth themselves.

Teens Supporting Bullied Peers

Ryan Walker was an average high school junior who wore many hats: she was a cheerleader, an honor roll student, and active in many clubs. On the surface, Walker seemed to be a well-adjusted teenager enjoying high school life, but in reality, she was being bullied.

One day during lunch, while talking to a cheerleader teammate, she discovered that she and a few others had been excluded from a team group chat. She brushed it off until a week later, when the same teammate told her that people were posting unflattering messages and videos about her in the chat. The friend showed her the posts. One was a picture of Walker walking through the cafeteria with a caption asking why she was around and "taking up oxygen."[14]

Walker tried to forget about these texts and videos, but her friend showed her that the other teammates continued posting more in the chat. These posts started to impact her. "I felt isolated and unwelcome while I constantly questioned if others around me shared the opinions of this one group," Walker writes. "I put on a brave face around school and tried to not let my anxiety show, but I would end my nights secretly in tears over the harsh things that were said. Only after confiding in my parents, did I understand and label this as bullying."[15]

"To break the cycle of bullying, it takes one person to step up and speak out."[16]

—Ryan Walker, teen victim of bullying

Walker eventually reported the bullying to the vice principal. After he talked to each girl in the text group, the bullying stopped. Walker believes it could have been stopped much earlier if her classmates had spoken up. While her friend did make her aware of the bullying, she did not do anything else. If the friend had vocally called out the others about the bullying or let an adult know, that would have been more impactful. Though this is not easy to do, studies have found that teens who speak out against bullying behavior can have a positive impact. According to the Tyler Clementi Foundation, a nonprofit antibullying organization, research shows that when bystanders intervene, 57 percent of the time bullying stops almost immediately.

Walker urges teens to take action if they become aware of a peer who is being bullied. "To break the cycle of bullying, it takes one person to step up and speak out. . . . Instead of standing by and hoping the problem will be fixed by someone else,"[16] she adds, teens need to learn to stand up for their peers who are being targeted by bullies.

Studies have found that teens who speak out against bullying behavior can have a positive impact. Research shows that when bystanders intervene, 57 percent of the time bullying stops immediately.

The Scope of the Problem

As Walker discovered, bullying can take many forms. Initially, she didn't realize she was being bullied. She thought of bullying in more traditional ways, such as verbal harassment and physical intimidation. However, after speaking with her parents, she recognized she had been bullied. The texting insults and sharing of derogatory pictures were cyberbullying, a type of bullying that is occurring with increasing frequency. According to a 2022 Pew Research Center survey, nearly half of US teens report having been victims of cyberbullying.

Cyberbullying occurs on social media platforms, through texting, and in online gaming messaging apps. The anonymity of the internet allows bullies to attack without fear of repercussion, making it easier for them to spread rumors, share humiliating photos, and exclude others from social circles. The result is similar to in-person bullying—victims are made to feel isolated, ashamed, and anxious.

The emotional and psychological toll of bullying can be severe. Research has shown that the experience of being bullied can lead to significant mental health challenges. Darby Fox, a licensed therapist, explains, "The experience and threat of bullying force the victim to be hyper-vigilant: their amygdala, the part of the brain responsible for our primal self-protective instincts known as 'fight-or-flight,' becomes overactive. This means that victims are likelier to experience anxiety and depression and have difficulty sleeping."[17]

Uplifting Others

Many young people do not report their experiences because they feel ashamed or embarrassed about being bullied. This often increases feelings of anxiety, depression, and isolation. But some teens have managed to overcome these feelings and joined efforts aimed at supporting victims and breaking the cycle of bullying. This is what Miah Green did.

Green was in elementary school when she experienced bullying. At age ten, Green had won an award for her volunteer work. She brought that award to school for show and tell. A classmate who heard Green's presentation called Green a liar and spread a story around school that the award was fake. After that several classmates started saying mean things to Green about her and about her award. There were many days when Green came home crying. She found she dreaded going back to school. The bullying she endured that year was mentally and emotionally exhausting.

The following year Green was homeschooled due to her schedule as an aerialist in a cirque troupe. Being homeschooled gave her a break from the bullying, and she gained her self-confidence back. She eventually realized she wanted to do something to prevent the same thing from happening to other kids. Green joined Free2Luv, a nonprofit organization dedicated to empowering students through the arts.

> **"The greatest reward is knowing that I planted a seed of hope in each young person's mind, being able to share my bullying story and helping today's youth see that they are unique, beautiful, strong and mostly, loved."[18]**
>
> —Miah Green, teen anti-bullying advocate

One of the group's goals is to help young people develop self-confidence so that they feel able to stand up to bullies. The group does this through school art programs that teach students creative ways to express themselves.

The group also has social media campaigns and podcasts aimed at young people. Green has shared her story and thoughts about empowerment in some of the group's podcasts and YouTube videos. She has even performed as an aerialist at Free2Luv events that focus on showing how visual and performance arts can uplift youth and give them confidence in themselves. "The greatest reward is knowing that I planted a seed of hope in each young person's mind, being able to share my bullying story and helping today's youth see that they are unique, beautiful, strong and mostly, loved,"[18] Green explains.

Targeted Groups

Certain groups of teens are at high risk of being bullied. One of these groups is LGBTQ young people. The Trevor Project surveyed more than eighteen thousand LGBTQ youth. Its report, published in 2024, found that 49 percent of thirteen- to seventeen-year-olds reported experiencing bullying in the previous year. The discrimination faced by LGBTQ youth can lead to severe emotional distress, including self-harm and thoughts of suicide. Similarly, 2022 research from the Pew Research Center indicates that teenage girls are more likely than other groups to experience cyberbullying. The survey revealed that 54 percent of girls aged fifteen to seventeen had encountered at least one form of online harassment, such as spreading false rumors or being targeted in group chats.

Anti-bullying Programs

While Free2Luv's focus is on helping students develop self-worth and self-confidence, other programs strive to provide young people with tools they can use to stop bullying. These programs teach teens how to recognize different forms of bullying—from physical or verbal harassment to online threats and social exclusion—and how to respond to it. They encourage teens to understand what people targeted by bullies are feeling. They also provide strategies that can be used to support victims.

PACER's National Bullying Prevention Center is an example of an organization that teaches teens to be anti-bullying advocates in their schools. One way they do this is to have students participate in various "What Should You Do?" activities. In one such activity, participants learn about a student with Down syndrome who has been surrounded by others who are mocking him. The participants then discuss possible reactions, ranging from ignoring what is happening to asking a teacher for help. They then consider the outcomes of these different responses.

This program emphasizes bystander intervention because research shows it can greatly reduce the frequency and impact of bullying incidents. Standing up against bullying can be intimidating. Sometimes teens fear that supporting a targeted peer might make them a new target, leading to ridicule or even physical aggression. This fear can deter them from intervening, even when they recognize that doing so is the right thing. The PACER program encourages young people to work together, since collective action often reduces individual vulnerability. The program emphasizes that if teens feel they are not alone, they are more likely to step in and support others.

Project Rockit, an Australia-based program, also does this. It teaches anti-bullying strategies through youth-led workshops. These workshops include group discussions and role-playing activities that teach teens practical skills for responding to bullying, supporting peers, and responsibly navigating social media. Project Rockit has reached thousands of students across Australia. Em, a

Sometimes teens fear that supporting a targeted peer might make them a new target. This fear can deter them from intervening, even when they recognize that doing so is the right thing.

Teaching Through Scenarios

In addition to school workshops, Project Rockit offers an online platform with youth-created videos that teach teens how to deal with real-life bullying scenarios. For example, one video shows what gamers can do if a player's anger morphs into messaged insults and bullying. The first suggestion is to simply not respond and continue playing. If the behavior continues, the video goes on to suggest, the targeted player should block the bully or report the bullying behavior to the game administrator or app administrator. And if players become angry and are tempted to respond with their own disparaging remarks, the video suggests reciting the alphabet backwards to give themselves time to calm down.

teen participant, shared her biggest takeaway from the program: "Definitely, be the solution. Always call out the behavior and know that the reward is bigger than the risk."[19]

Strength from Others

For some teens, the personal experiences shared by others are what helps them deal with their own bullying situation. Jay Taylor, an LGBTQ and biracial teen, experienced bullying from classmates. In eighth grade, an anonymous Facebook group of classmates formed to target Taylor online. The group added swastikas to Taylor's photos and mocked every detail of Taylor's appearance. The online posts grew much darker when the group added references to suicide. According to Taylor, many classmates participated in the online harassment, which eventually reached the point that authorities had to get involved.

At the time, what gave Taylor strength to go forward was watching the *It Gets Better* video by singer Adam Lambert. In the video, Lambert talks about his own struggles with being bullied as an LGBTQ person. It Gets Better is an organization dedicated to empowering and connecting lesbian, gay, bisexual, transgender, and queer youth around the globe. Its large online library includes many videos in which celebrities share their ex-

Singer Adam Lambert has been open about his struggles being bullied growing up as an LGBTQ person. He has been an inspiration to LGBTQ teens struggling to overcome their challenges.

periences of overcoming challenges related to sexual orientation or gender identity. These videos aim to show young viewers that struggles are temporary and that life can and does improve with time. Lambert also sought to show young people that they are not alone and that they do not simply have to endure. They can thrive. This message resonated with Taylor, who after years of self-discovery in high school and college eventually became a graphic art designer with the It Gets Better organization.

Being part of an organization that helps teens stand up for themselves and push back against negativity makes Taylor proud. "After growing up in environments that sought to suppress aspects of my identity, I now have the privilege of shaping the visual identity of an organization that helped me stay strong during a period of bullying and isolation,"[20] says Taylor.

Teen Initiatives

In addition to joining anti-bullying organizations, many teens have taken it upon themselves to create their own initiatives that combat bullying and promote kindness. One such group was created by students at San Clemente High School in California. The group, Cool 2 Be Kind, formed after the tragic suicide of a classmate who had endured years of bullying. The student-run club hosts various events and encourages students to share their experiences. As an example, the group organizes an annual anti-bullying march in nearby Laguna Beach, where students come together to raise awareness and show solidarity against bullying. The group also conducts a Blue Ribbon Week, which includes themed activities such as making a compliment wall, where students post kind messages and compliments about their peers.

> **"Before experiencing bullying, I was . . . naïve about the reality of how bullying affects someone. Like too many, I was one who thought if you were 'strong enough,' or just had the right attitude, you could shrug it off and not be hurt by others' words and actions. This is SO far from the truth."[21]**
>
> —Jamie, a teen who was bullied

Another student-run initiative was created by Jamie, a teen who says she faced vicious bullying from a school classmate. In an effort to help others, she created a public blog to share her experiences. Jamie says:

> Before experiencing bullying, I was . . . naïve about the reality of how bullying affects someone. Like too many, I was one who thought if you were "strong enough," or just had the right attitude, you could shrug it off and not be hurt by others' words and actions. This is SO far from the truth, as I learned the hard way. I learned that no matter how much confidence or strength someone has, one can still be hurt by someone's actions and words and still be strong—it does not suddenly mean you are weak! It means you are human.[21]

To help others, Jamie decided to open up about her experience and answer questions from peers on how to recognize, deal with, and stand up for others affected by bullying. From 2017 to 2021, she became a go-to resource for her peers, hosting a blog on the Teens Against Bullying website. People could write in and she would answer their questions. In one exchange, a teen talked about being the target of hurtful gossip. Jamie emphasized that the treatment the teen was experiencing was indeed bullying. She acknowledged that there is often a stigma surrounding the term *bullying*, which can lead teens to minimize the severity of their experiences. This stigma makes it painful for victims to accept their situation and can instill fear in them regarding the use of the term, complicating their ability to recognize and confront the issue. Jamie's message to this teen and many others was that there is no shame in being bullied—it is the bully who is in the wrong.

Being Strong

Fighting against the bullying of peers is not easy. Whether personally speaking out or working with an organization, it takes courage to do what's right. When a teen wrote in to ask Jamie about what she should do when one of her friends was insulting and bullying another, Jamie responded that the right choice is always to stand up for the one being bullied. "Don't be accusatory or mean; simply say something like, 'I don't appreciate how you are talking about my friend. I am concerned you don't realize how hurtful your words can be, since if you did, I believe you would stop,'"[22] advised Jamie. She went on to suggest that if this action did not work, or the person asking for advice did not feel safe acting, to involve an adult, emphasizing that is not tattling but keeping another from hurtful behavior.

Teens who engage in anti-bullying efforts face unique challenges, like the fear of retaliation and potential social isolation. Despite these obstacles, their involvement can foster a culture of kindness and support that benefits the whole community. By advocating for their peers and actively working to counter bullying, teens create safer, more inclusive environments. These initiatives not only empower them personally but also inspire others to stand up for kindness and create an environment where bullying is less common.

Teens Tutoring Teens

Marcus C. was failing his advanced biology class. His teacher was frequently absent, and the substitute teacher provided minimal assistance. Marcus needed help and needed it quickly. He discovered Schoolhouse.world, an online peer-to-peer tutoring service. After signing up, he was matched with a peer tutor. "My tutor was the best. He never missed a day and was on time. His PowerPoints were clear and concise," Marcus writes. "I understood lessons, learned without all of the distractions, and he took his time. Instead of taking a bunch of notes, I was able to learn and get a clear explanation of each lesson."[23] At the end of the term, Marcus took the exam and got a good grade on it. Peer tutoring provided him with the extra attention and explanations he needed to succeed.

Marcus is just one of many teens who has needed extra help with academics and has benefited from the assistance of peer tutors. For some students, like Marcus, science classes are a hurdle. Other students encounter challenges in English, history, math, foreign languages, computer education, and other classes. Peer tutors offer academic help to students with various needs.

Understanding the Need for Peer Tutoring

Academically, today's teenagers face numerous challenges. Recent data from the National Center for Education Statistics reveal that a significant portion of students struggle with core subjects. In 2021 approximately 28 percent of eighth-grade students performed below the basic level in mathematics, while 21 percent were below the basic level in reading.

The COVID-19 pandemic that began in 2020 further intensified these challenges. Nationwide, students fell behind in reading and math due to many schools closing and moving to remote schedules. A 2022 study conducted by the Center for Education Policy Research examined data from twenty-nine states and found that public school students in grades three to eight experienced significant learning losses during the pandemic. When comparing post-pandemic assessment results from 2022 to pre-pandemic assessments from 2019, the study estimated that students lost the equivalent of a half year of learning in math and a quarter year in reading.

One effective response to these challenges is peer tutoring. Teens are uniquely suited to help one another overcome academic obstacles, offering support that is relatable and affordable. The shared experiences and language between students who need help and students who give help create an environment conducive to learning and growth. In 2019 Ava Hazzouri, then a high school sophomore in Kingston, Pennsylvania, launched a peer tutoring program after she had experienced the benefits of one-on-one tutoring. Her program, the Study Hard Project, is

Peer tutors offer academic help to students with various needs. Teens are uniquely suited to help one another overcome academic obstacles, offering support that is relatable and affordable.

run by students from Northeastern Pennsylvania and offers both online and in-person tutoring. Hazzouri has witnessed positive outcomes among her peers. Hazzouri explains:

> Peer tutoring is an actionable, cost-effective (often, free!) way to level the academic playing field for middle and high school students across the country. The best part is that when students help students, everyone benefits. Research shows that peer tutoring leads to an increase in academic performance, school attendance, socialization, self-esteem, and attitude toward school for all involved, and I can attest to all of it![24]

Why It Works

Peer tutoring serves as a powerful tool for students struggling academically by creating an environment where they feel more comfortable seeking help. Many teens find the formal teacher-student relationship of professional tutoring to be intimidating—and too expensive. In contrast, peer tutoring breaks down these barriers, fostering a supportive environment that allows for relaxed communication and learning.

> **"She understood what I was talking about when I told her the problems I was having because she had taken this same class too."[25]**
>
> —Mayda Murillo, recipient of peer tutoring

For Mayda Murillo, a senior at Caldwell High School in Idaho, being tutored by her friend, Ashley Cardona, led to significant improvements in her algebra class. Murillo credits the comfortable learning environment, where Cardona could relate to her experiences in the class. After her algebra grade dropped to a D, Murillo knew she needed help. Asking a classmate for help seemed easier than seeking a teacher's assistance. "I knew Ashley and felt comfortable with her," Murillo says. "She understood what I was talking about when I told her the problems I was having because she had taken this same class too."[25] Peer tutoring helped Murillo build confidence and realize what she could achieve with extra instruction and encouragement.

The peer-to-peer dynamic is a key factor in the success of these programs. Since the tutor and the student being tutored are close in age and educational experience, they share an understanding of the challenges each faces. Peer tutors have recently covered the same material, enabling them to explain difficult concepts in ways that resonate with their peers. This sense of empathy, often missing in professional tutoring services in which the tutor may not fully relate to the teen experience, allows students to feel less embarrassed about making mistakes and encourages open dialogue. Ava Hazzouri, founder of the Study Hard Project, observed that many students feel more comfortable asking questions of their peers than their teachers. "Students have shared that learning from their peers feels less threatening for them than asking for teachers' help," Hazzouri explains. "One student said he feels awkward asking teachers his questions because he worries they'll get mad that he wasn't listening in class."[26] This lack of fear is a crucial aspect of peer tutoring's success.

Types of Tutoring

Peer tutoring can take many forms. One-on-one tutoring provides a personalized experience, allowing students to focus on their specific academic needs. For example, Cardona's one-on-one work with Murillo helped her review concepts and prepare for tests. After spending a week working with Cardona, Murillo earned a B on her test, a significant improvement from the grades she had been getting.

Group tutoring is another option. In this setup, a tutor helps multiple students simultaneously, enabling them to work together on concepts and problems. Another advantage of group tutoring is that it allows students to realize they are not alone in their academic struggles.

The rise of online peer tutoring has opened new opportunities for students needing help. Platforms like Teens Tutor Teens and Schoolhouse.world make it easy for students to connect virtually and receive real-time support. Bianca C., a high school student

Cross-Cultural Help

Many students who arrive in the United States from other countries face significant challenges learning English during their first few years of school. To support these students, AIMS College Prep Middle School in Oakland, California, has developed a peer tutoring program that pairs English language learners with bilingual peers. Peer tutors, who often share cultural or linguistic backgrounds with their partnered students, help strengthen reading, writing, and conversational English skills. Sessions typically last thirty minutes and take place several days a week. Working together, either one-on-one or in small groups, tutors and students focus on practical exercises like reading together, practicing vocabulary, and conversational role-playing.

Beyond improving language skills, the program fosters valuable interaction between students. "This has led to awesome cross-cultural friendships," notes program coordinator Adria Banihashemi. Both tutors and learners benefit: tutors gain leadership and communication skills, while the English language learners develop confidence and academic competence. The program exemplifies how collaboration and peer support can transform the learning experience for all involved.

Quoted in Jonathon Zabala, "How Peer Teaching Assistants Can Support Multilingual Learners," Edutopia, March 26, 2023. www.edutopia.org.

who used Schoolhouse.world for SAT math preparation, shared how her online peer tutor helped her overcome challenges in trigonometry. "I used to think I would never be able to solve a trigonometry problem," Bianca says. During one of her practice tests, she froze when she encountered a triangle problem, but then she recalled a memory aid her tutor had taught her for that type of problem. "I solved the problem by applying what I learned. Even though I didn't get the question right due to forgetting to simplify the answer, my tutor and I were proud of the progress I made. I was proud of solving something I never thought I could solve."[27] For Bianca, working with a peer who understood what she was learning and the convenience of online sessions led to greater confidence and capability in the subject.

> "I was proud of solving something I never thought I could solve."[27]
>
> —Bianca C., recipient of peer tutoring

Impact of Peer Tutoring

Peer tutoring has proved to be a valuable experience for both the students who tutor and the students who receive help, leading to academic improvement and personal growth. Learning from peers often makes students feel more comfortable, promoting success in multiple areas, from grades to self-confidence. Tutors also gain confidence by realizing they can help others, often growing personally as they connect with their peers and learning to understand others' struggles.

Academically, peer tutoring has been shown to lead to higher grades and pass rates. At North Star Academy in Newark, New Jersey, principal Michael Mann observed that about 54 percent of students who were peer tutored passed a class in the second

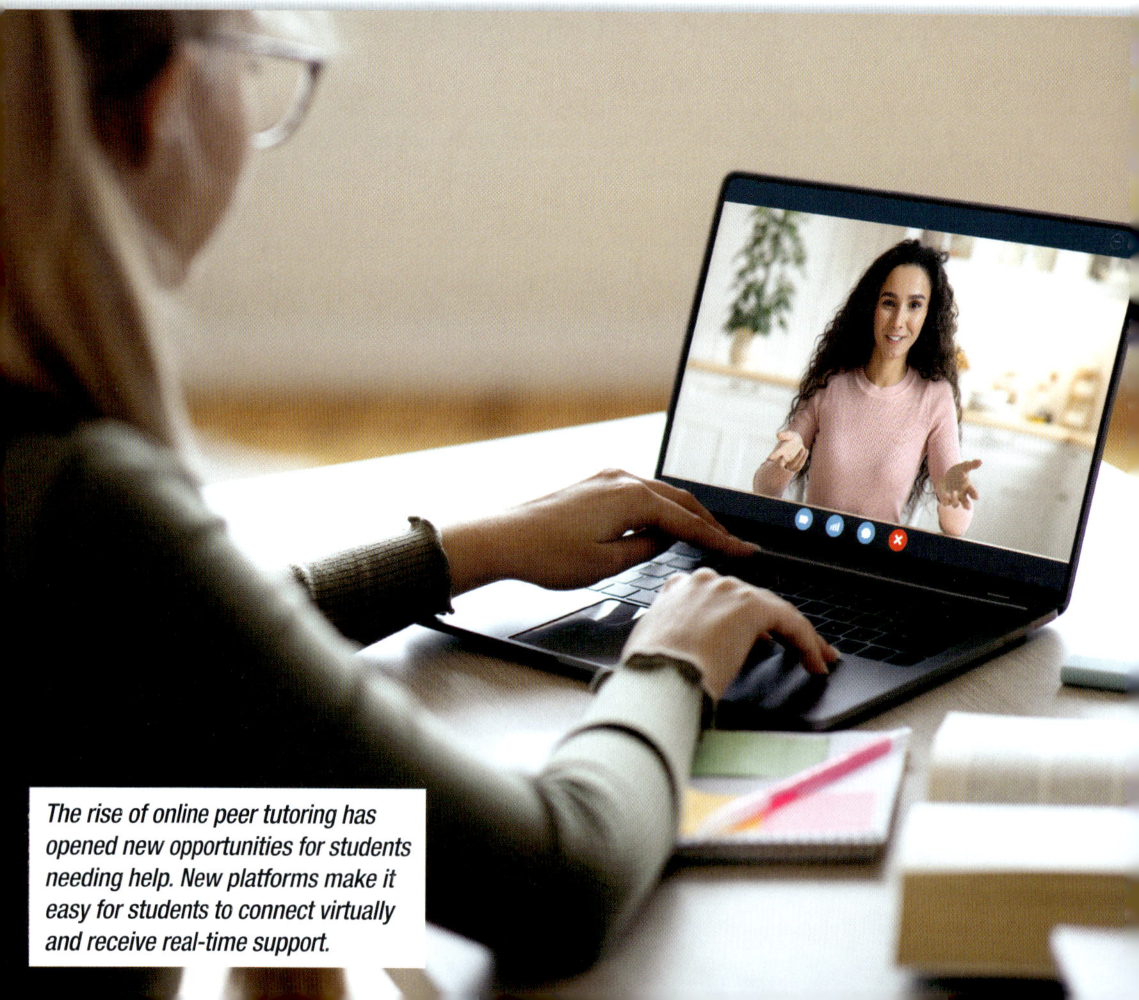

The rise of online peer tutoring has opened new opportunities for students needing help. New platforms make it easy for students to connect virtually and receive real-time support.

quarter after failing it in the first. The Study Hard Project has seen similar results among those tutored. Hazzouri shared, "One of our eighth graders told us that he went from a 54 percent average to a 91 percent in math from participating in weekly tutoring with us."[28]

> **"Working with Study Hard, I've learned that empowering others is the best way to feel my own power."[29]**
>
> —Shawna, tutor at Study Hard Project

Research from the Education Endowment Foundation, a UK nonprofit focused on breaking the link between family income and educational outcomes, supports the idea that peer tutoring not only improves grades but also accelerates learning. Studies from the foundation show that students in peer tutoring programs can advance their learning by an additional five months over an academic year.

Peer tutoring benefits more than just academic performance. Many tutors talk about how they develop confidence from helping fellow students. Shawna, a tutor from Wyoming Seminary Upper School, reflected, "Working with Study Hard, I've learned that empowering others is the best way to feel my own power."[29] For Shawna, helping others has become a way to develop leadership skills and boost her own self-confidence. Molly, a tutor from Scranton Preparatory School, shared a similar sentiment, stating that tutoring helped her realize she is smart and capable of teaching others. Peer tutoring allows students to take ownership of their knowledge and become leaders in their academic communities.

Connections

Another benefit of peer tutoring is that it fosters a sense of community among youth who might not usually interact. Helping peers reach their goals helps build a closer, more meaningful connection between students. Romina A., who tutors students on improving SAT scores through Schoolhouse.world, became a tutor after getting help through the same program. Romina writes, "Helping another student reach their 'Aha!' moment when it comes to learning is an incredible sense of fulfillment I get to

Tutor Training

The most effective peer tutoring programs include training for teen tutors. Teens who want to become peer tutors through the online Schoohouse. world program, for example, attend informational sessions with experienced tutors, complete various training modules, and take online certification tests to ensure knowledge in specific subject areas. Prospective tutors also learn how to connect with learners, how to communicate respectfully and safely, and how to make tutoring sessions fun as well as beneficial for students. Even after tutoring sessions begin, tutors have access to ongoing support from a community of fellow high school tutors and experienced coaches. They are there to answer questions and share helpful tips and techniques. It is with training like this that both tutors and learners can achieve success.

experience with each session I host. On top of that, I get to meet well-rounded, passionate students from all over the world, some from Korea, France, Canada, Brazil, South Africa, and Nigeria."[30]

Kevin Buanga, a thirteen-year-old at Ockerman Middle School in Kentucky, tutors students with special needs. He says that he has been profoundly affected by his interactions with these students. Having immigrated from Congo and learning English in the United States as a child, Buanga understands what it is to feel different. This experience led him to sign up to be a peer tutor for students who have moderate to severe disabilities. He helps them in a class that teaches both academics and life skills.

Buanga views each student as a unique individual. To know best how to work with the students, he pays close attention to what they say and how they feel. For example, he created secret handshakes to better connect with one student. He fostered a connection with another student by playing with Barbie dolls. The teachers he works with note that he has learned to observe the class and knows when to jump in to help if students do not understand something. Buanga hopes his friends learn to be more inclusive of students who may be different by observing how he interacts with the students he tutors. "I would like [my friends] to put themselves in [the special needs students'] shoes and imagine how that kid feels whenever . . . a kid walks by and sees them and starts laughing,"[31] Buanga says. Through tutoring, Buanga has not only helped his peers improve their skills and confidence, he has also become more compassionate and developed his own leadership abilities.

As Buanga discovered, peer tutoring is a powerful educational tool with meaningful impacts on both tutors and students who receive help. Whether it's improving pass rates, boosting grades, accelerating learning, or fostering personal growth, peer tutoring extends beyond the classroom. It empowers teens to succeed academically while growing as individuals, proving that learning and teaching can be equally rewarding.

Teen Mentors

Starting college, particularly away from home and all that is familiar, is exciting but can also be scary and overwhelming. Izzy, a freshman at the University of Bristol in the United Kingdom, found that her transition to university life was made smoother because she had a mentor. Mentors at the University of Bristol are students who have attended the school for at least a year and are there to help new students navigate both the academic and social aspects of university life. "[My mentor] was super helpful at [explaining] what the university had to offer and where to find it,"[32] she says. Two years later, she and her mentor were still close, having formed a bond during that first year.

Peer mentoring involves teens helping other teens adjust to new situations or provide support and encouragement when such things are in short supply. Typically, the teen mentor has experienced the same situation or felt the same need for encouragement as the teen who is on the receiving end. That is the value of teens mentoring teens: the mentors understand how it feels to be new or in an unfamiliar place around unfamiliar people or just need a little extra support—because they too have experienced these feelings.

Transitions

Life transitions, like starting college or moving to a new city or country, can be disorienting. This is especially true when few of the people around you seem to have had similar life experiences or have come from very different backgrounds. Some universities, for instance, do not have a diverse racial and ethnic mix among their students. Knowing how disorienting it can be for students to arrive at a university and not see many people who look like them, some schools have established mentorship programs for students of various ethnicities.

The University of Virginia (UVA), for instance, offers these types of peer mentor programs. In these programs, new students are paired with a group of peer mentors who have a similar ethnic background. The mentors have completed at least one year at the college and have also gone through the mentoring program. The group serves as an on-campus support network, which helps the new student acclimate to school and feel at home. Throughout the year, they might get together for meals, sporting events, and other social activities. Sarai Villagomez, who became a mentor after benefiting from the program during her first year, explains, "A lot of minorities and people of color feel like they don't see people like them at UVA, and by being able to match them with someone who has similar experiences as them, it makes them feel more comfortable."[33]

"A lot of minorities and people of color feel like they don't see people like them at UVA, and by being able to match them with someone who has similar experiences as them, it makes them feel more comfortable."[33]

—Sarai Villagomez, University of Virginia mentee and mentor

Peer mentoring involves teens helping other teens adjust to new situations such as a new college campus.

Augusta University in Georgia has also developed peer programs to support students from diverse backgrounds. Like at UVA, Augusta's mentoring program helps students navigate both academic and personal challenges. Mentors share their experiences, offer advice, and help students feel more connected to the university community.

Finding Connections

Among the most valuable aspects of mentorship programs, according to those who have taken part in them, are the personal connections they create. Gracyn Bennett, a first-generation college student, struggled with academics and friendships during her freshman year. During that year, Bennett often retreated to her apartment, staying in her room rather than engaging in social activities. Her social life expanded when she joined a sorority, but she still had difficulty adjusting academically. Four years later she reflects on how a mentor would have made her first year easier. "For me, I feel like it was difficult to adjust to my classes that first

Teaching Empathy

Peer programs typically provide training to mentors on how to establish and maintain positive, supportive relationships with their assigned students. With Link Crew, the leader-mentors attend workshops focused on developing leadership skills, empathy, and effective communication. The training is interactive. It often includes role-playing activities in which upperclassmen practice guiding their peers through common high school challenges like navigating schedules, balancing homework, and social pressure. As Link Crew leader Kyia Sparks said of the training, "I really enjoyed learning all the fun games that we get to do because it's just us playing for a little bit but we're also learning how to teach the freshmen as well." Leaders are trained to recognize signs of bullying or anxiety among their students and know how to step in with support. This preparation helps create strong, supportive relationships between mentors and their mentees, laying the foundation for a smoother transition to high school.

Quoted in Claire Bauer, "Link Crew Leads the Way," Rock Media, August 17, 2023. https://rockmediaonline.org.

Among the most valuable aspects of mentorship programs, according to those who have taken part in them, are the personal connections they create.

year because high school does not prepare you whatsoever for college," she says. "I know that they try to, but nothing can ever prepare you. And I was really struggling with my science classes my first year. I wish I had someone like a mentor to guide me. I kind of just got thrown into the fishbowl and had to figure it out myself."[34]

Bennett's experience led her to apply as a mentor in the Jags4Jags program, which matches upperclassmen with new students with similar interests and fields of study. In 2024 Bennett was paired with Angel Lexley, a first-year kinesiology student from Savannah, Georgia. Lexley knew no one on campus, so meeting Bennett helped ease her transition. Both were from Savannah, Georgia, and shared similar academic and athletic interests. And like Bennett, Lexley was the first person in her family to attend college. These shared experiences created an immediate bond. "I think that first night when we went to the Welcome Back Bash, we just connected," Lexley says. "We had dinner, we talked, and it felt really natural. It was like hanging out with somebody that I pretty much knew my whole life."[35] The mentorship experience helped relieve some of the anxieties Lexley felt about being the first in her family to attend college. She was able to ask Bennett for advice on classes and activities, but the two also engaged in deeper conversations about their shared faith and beliefs. By blending academic guidance with personal support, mentors like Bennett ensure that new students feel supported and cared for.

High School Student Support

Peer mentorship programs supporting transitioning students are not limited to the college level. Many high schools have also implemented such programs to assist incoming students with the academic and social challenges. One well-known national program, Link Crew, focuses on helping incoming ninth graders feel comfortable and supported throughout their first year.

Link Crew operates in 3,705 schools across forty-seven states and is based on the belief that students are well suited to help their peers navigate challenges. In the program, juniors and seniors are trained as Link Crew leaders. The leaders act as mentors to freshmen, providing guidance and encouragement to help them face the ups and downs of that first year of high school. At Amity Regional High School in Woodbridge, Connecticut, senior Sadie Chadbourne remembers how her own Link Crew leader eased her anxiety as a freshman by helping her navigate her first day. Now a Link Leader herself, Chadbourne explains, "My link crew leader . . . waited by the front of the school to walk me to that classroom and I wanted to do that for other kids that have bad anxiety as well."[36] The Link Crew mentors also make themselves available to all new students, not just the students who are assigned to them. In the initial weeks, they wear Link Crew shirts so students

> **"My link crew leader . . . waited by the front of the school to walk me to that classroom and I wanted to do that for other kids that have bad anxiety as well."[36]**
>
> —Sadie Chadbourne, Link Crew mentee

Academic Success

Peer mentoring programs have been found to boost academic performance for students by providing support from experienced peers. According to a 2024 research paper by Jennifer Graham and colleagues from Colorado State University, peer mentorship enhanced students' sense of investment in college activities, leading to greater academic success. Mentors often assist with homework, share study techniques, and offer guidance on how to balance schoolwork with other responsibilities. Alina Cuellar was initially reluctant to have a mentor when she started Western Governors University, an online university based in Southern California. Initially, she says, she did not see the need. Cuellar soon realized the positive effect working with a mentor could have on her academics. "She kept me on track and organized," Cuellar says. "Emily listened to everything I had questions or comments about. She is the reason I stayed in school towards the end."

Quoted in WGU, "Why WGU Students Rave About Their Mentors," June 10, 2022. www.wgu.edu.

know they're available to answer questions, from finding classrooms to learning school routines.

Throughout the year, Link Leaders connect with the students they are mentoring in various ways. They visit their classrooms to check on academic progress. They meet for informal get-togethers and attend social events together. These gatherings offer students a chance to relax and have fun together.

Matthew Muravnik was hesitant to take part in his high school's many social activities in his freshman year. But his Link Crew mentor encouraged him to get involved—and he did. Reflecting on his high school experience, Muravnik says, "Now as a senior . . . I see how important it is to attend these events . . . we're not going to be here [forever], and you want to look back and have fond memories of high school."[37] Ultimately, Link Crew's goal is to foster a supportive student community that increases attendance, reduces disciplinary issues, and enhances academic and social outcomes for high school students. The connections between the upperclassmen and freshmen are key to these goals.

Different Learners

Youth mentoring programs also support preteens and teens with special needs, focusing on uplifting students who may face unique academic or social challenges. Students with special needs often learn differently, which can lead to feelings of isolation and anxiety in traditional educational settings. Peer mentoring can provide valuable support. A prominent national program, Eye to Eye, pairs middle school students who learn differently with high school and college mentors who have navigated similar challenges.

Eye to Eye serves fifth- to eighth-grade students in over one thousand schools nationwide. In weekly after-school sessions, mentors engage with their assigned students in creative activities that build social skills and teach them how to advocate for themselves. Mentors are carefully matched with students based on shared experiences and learning styles, creating an environment where students feel understood and valued.

David Flink, the program's founder, was diagnosed with ADHD and dyslexia at age eleven. His parents' support helped him manage school and eventually graduate, but it wasn't until college that he met other students with similar learning differences. Together, they began a mentoring program for local elementary students facing similar challenges, sparking the idea for Eye to Eye. Today thousands of youth benefit from the program. Its surveys show that 87 percent of students who were mentored through Eye to Eye felt more positive about their future, and 82 percent looked up to their mentors as role models. "Eye to Eye has been huge to my personal development," says Cassidy Wald, an Eye to Eye alum. "Having a community where I could talk openly about my learning differences and feel empowered as a self-advocate . . . was so important on my journey."[38]

> **"I like being there to show them it is OK to have learning disabilities . . . you're going to make it. It's going to be OK."[39]**
>
> —Morgan Silverman, Eye to Eye mentor

Participants in the Eye to Eye mentor program at AIM Academy in Pennsylvania have also found the experience rewarding. AIM Academy is a K–12 school that specializes in students

Youth mentoring programs also support preteens and teens with special needs, focusing on uplifting students who may face unique academic or social challenges.

who learn differently and deal with challenges such as dyslexia, autism, and ADHD. Susan Carson, AIM's faculty mentor, has seen students grow through interactions with their mentors. Mentors like high school students Morgan Silverman and Maddie White, both chapter leaders for the 2022–2023 school year, participated in weekly art sessions with students in the program. The mentors guided the students through projects that fostered confidence and skills. Silverman explained her motivation for joining the program. "I like being there to show them it is OK to have learning disabilities . . . you're going to make it. It's going to be OK,"[39] she says.

Both Silverman and Carson particularly liked the activities that led to self-reflection. One memorable activity, Lily Pads, involved students decorating pads with words of encouragement. They then placed the pads on the floor and hopped from pad to pad as if they were using lily pads to hop across a river or pond. This exercise is a metaphor for relying on different supports to overcome obstacles.

Programs like Eye to Eye demonstrate the power of peer mentoring in creating inclusive environments where all students can thrive. The students learn they are not alone, and together they navigate the challenges and transitions in their lives.

Mental Health Help

Ava Peterson, an eighth grader and member of the Hope Squad, a peer-to-peer program that trains students in mental health support skills, received a concerning message during spring break. One of Peterson's friends thought another friend might be in trouble because she seemed depressed. Peterson's friend messaged that she did not know what to do but thought that Peterson would. Through Hope Squad at her school in Crystal Lake, Texas, Peterson had received training in how to spot warning signs of a mental health crisis, how to approach peers, and whom to refer them to in case of a concern.

Peterson immediately acted. "It was over spring break, so there were no trusted adults at school that I could talk to," she says. "So, I ended up calling for a wellness check just to make sure that person was okay."[40] A friend or relative who is worried about someone's safety and cannot reach the person directly can contact a local law enforcement agency to request a wellness check. A wellness check is intended to verify the individual's general safety and well-being. Peterson found that her classmate was doing okay and not in crisis. After spring break, Peterson talked to a school counselor to ensure another person checked in on her classmate. Actions like hers are helping prevent crises among young people.

Peterson's friend is not unique. According to the National Institute of Mental Health, about one in five teens experiences a mental health disorder each year. These disorders range from anxiety and depression to eating disorders and suicidal thoughts. The COVID-19 pandemic further worsened the situation; emergency room visits for mental health–related crises among adolescents aged twelve to seventeen surged by 31 percent in 2020 compared to 2019. This spike reflects the toll the pandemic has taken on young people, leaving them feeling isolated and anxious. And although the pandemic has passed, mental health among youth is still a major issue. According to the Centers for Disease Control and Prevention's latest Youth Risk Behavior Survey, in 2023, 39.7 percent of high school students reported persistently feeling sad or hopeless in the past year, compared to 36.7 percent in 2019.

With so many young people experiencing mental health struggles, peer help is one critical aspect of dealing with this problem. Because she was trained, Peterson knew her friend needed help. Peers like Peterson are often the first to notice signs of distress in others, so teen-to-teen support can have a major positive impact.

Scope of the Crisis

While all teens are susceptible to mental health challenges, certain groups face unique struggles. LGBTQ youth are especially vulnerable, often experiencing discrimination, bullying, and

Studies show that about one in five teens experiences a mental health disorder each year. These disorders range from anxiety and depression to eating disorders and suicidal thoughts.

family rejection. A 2022 study by the Trevor Project found that 45 percent of LGBTQ teens had seriously considered suicide in the past year, highlighting the need for targeted peer support for this population.

Teens of color also encounter distinct mental health challenges, often due to systemic racism and disparities in access to mental health care. For example, Black teens may experience heightened anxiety and fear when interacting with law enforcement. Black drivers are 20 percent more likely to be stopped by police than White drivers, based on a 2019 study by the Stanford Open Policing Project. Another issue for Black and Hispanic youth is that getting access to care for mental health issues can be a struggle. According to a 2021 report by the American Academy of Pediatrics, Black and Hispanic teens are less likely to receive mental health services despite experiencing higher rates of trauma.

Additionally, young teenage girls are particularly prone to mental health issues, especially anxiety and depression, due to outside pressures. The pressures of social media and body image concerns disproportionately affect them. In 2021 the Centers for Disease Control and Prevention reported that 37 percent of girls aged twelve to seventeen experienced depressive symptoms, nearly twice the rate of boys in the same age group.

Caring for Yourself

When helping peers through mental health challenges, maintaining healthy boundaries is important to protect your own well-being. Remember that you are there to support, not solve a friend's problems. While the desire to help can be strong, becoming overly involved in someone else's struggles can lead to emotional burnout or feelings of helplessness. Setting boundaries can mean limiting the amount of time spent discussing difficult topics or taking breaks from emotionally intense conversations. It can also mean limiting how often you see each other or text. To maintain boundaries and protect your emotional energy, step back and encourage friends to seek help from others such as school counselors or mental health professionals. It is also important to regularly check in with an adult mentor or counselor who can help you process the emotions you have while helping others.

Among these targeted groups and all other teens, mental health issues manifest in various forms. Depression is one of the most common, often appearing as persistent sadness, withdrawal, or loss of interest in activities. Another prevalent issue is anxiety, which can result in overwhelming worry or panic attacks. Other mental health concerns include eating disorders, self-harm, and suicidal ideation. Youth today need support to address these struggles, and their peers can play a vital role in providing help.

Why Teens Can Help

Teens often connect with each other in ways that adults cannot. The middle and high school years are typically filled with intense emotional changes and social challenges, and many teens feel more understood by their peers than by adults. According to Mental Health America, a nonprofit dedicated to promoting mental health, "Peers are important for teens since they often turn to their peers for support before anyone else. Peer support can be especially helpful for youth from historically excluded communities. They may face challenges that others cannot relate to because they have not experienced them. But peers can fill that gap."[41] The shared understanding among teens makes it easier for them to discuss their feelings, struggles, or mental health issues.

> **"Peers are important for teens since they often turn to their peers for support before anyone else. Peer support can be especially helpful for youth from historically excluded communities."[41]**
>
> —Mental Health America

Being able to confide in a friend is how Tara, as a junior in high school, started to find a path out of her depression. During the school year, Tara, previously a top-performing student, suddenly found her class load overwhelming and started struggling with schoolwork and experiencing other personal challenges. She lost all interest in even trying to keep up in school. And then she began to withdraw from family and friends. This situation eventually led to a deep depression. It was not until Tara confided in a close friend that things began to improve. Sharing her struggles, especially with someone who understood the

The middle and high school years are typically filled with intense emotional changes and social challenges, and many teens feel more understood by their peers than by adults.

pressures that she was undergoing, lifted an enormous weight. "Talking to my friend made me realize that people really do care,"[42] Tara says. This connection became a turning point, because Tara no longer felt completely alone.

Tara's friend listened without judgment, providing a sense of support that adults might not have been able to offer. Tara recognized that while life is full of challenges, opening up to someone can make all the difference. This moment of peer support emphasizes how teens can be integral in helping one another through mental health struggles.

Reaching Out

Many teens are stepping up to support their peers' mental health by joining or forming organizations aimed at suicide prevention and crisis intervention. Programs like Hope Squad train students in mental health awareness and provide them with tools to create support networks.

Hope Squad operates in over sixteen hundred schools across the United States and Canada. It focuses on equipping students with the skills to recognize signs of depression, anxiety, and suicidal thoughts among classmates. Squad members receive training in active listening (a communication skill that involves fully concentrating on, understanding, and responding to what another is saying), problem solving, and emotional support and are instructed to contact an adult immediately if they suspect a peer may be at risk for self-harm. By learning how to identify warning signs like behavioral or mood changes, Hope Squad members become a crucial first line of support, helping prevent crises through early intervention.

Eighth grader Millie Ferretti, a Hope Squad member, joined to be a friend and ally to classmates in need. She believes that teens may feel more comfortable approaching peers rather than adults because they feel less judgment. "I feel like it's easier to talk to your friends in some situations because you're around your friends a lot and you know and trust them," she explains. "With teachers, it's more like they're there to teach you, and it can be hard to talk to them sometimes because they're a lot older than you."[43]

"I feel like it's easier to talk to your friends in some situations because you're around your friends a lot and you know and trust them."[43]

—Millie Ferretti, a Hope Squad member

Similarly, Aidan became a mental health advocate in high school after witnessing his close family friend Hana's mental health crisis during the COVID-19 lockdown. Hana had been battling depression, which worsened with isolation. Unaware of her condition's severity, Aidan initially avoided her, thinking she just had a negative attitude. When Hana eventually required emergency intervention, Aidan realized the importance of recognizing mental health issues. After hospitalization and eventual psychological treatment, Hana improved, but Aidan wished he had supported her earlier. This led to him joining Teen Lifeline, a peer-supported crisis hotline in Arizona. Aidan underwent a seventy-two-hour training course to become a certified peer counselor. This training includes intensive workshops that

When to Get Immediate Help

There are times when good intentions and thoughtful support are not enough. If a classmate is showing signs of being in crisis—such as expressing suicidal thoughts, talking about self-harm, or showing severe emotional distress—it's crucial to act quickly. The first step is to remain calm and listen without judgment. Make it clear that you are concerned about your classmate's safety and are there to help. Try not to leave the person alone. If you think a peer may be at risk or in the process of preparing to attempt suicide, "you no longer have time or the luxury to get their opinion," says Justin Baker, clinical director of the Suicide and Trauma Reduction Initiative for Veterans at Ohio State University Wexner Medical Center. It's better to take action than wait to see whether the person is truly suicidal. Immediately contact a trusted adult. This could be a school counselor, teacher, or parent. If you cannot get an adult involved right away, call 988, the Suicide & Crisis Lifeline, or even emergency services (911) if necessary.

Quoted in Kristen Rogers, "People Who Attempt Suicide Might Show Signs Early On. Here's What to Watch For," CNN, December 15, 2022. www.cnn.com.

teach the active-listening, problem-solving, and decision-making skills necessary to handle crisis calls effectively.

Aidan now volunteers with Teen Lifeline, providing vital support to teens in crisis. "It's not easy to listen to someone in pain," Aidan shares, "but knowing I can make a difference is why I keep going."[44] Now serving as part of the Governor's Youth Commission for teen mental health, Aidan remains passionate about helping other teens find hope.

Mental Health First Aid

Some schools even offer courses for students who want to learn how to help peers who are experiencing emotional difficulties. One such course, Teen Mental Health First Aid, was developed by the National Council for Mental Wellbeing. Designed for high school students, it teaches them how to spot and support a peer who might be struggling with a mental health or substance use issue. Those who complete the course become, in a sense, first responders. They learn to assess a situation, do what they can in the moment, and inform a trusted adult. The course covers areas such as anxiety and panic disorders, depression, suicide, eating disorders, addiction, and other mental health problems that frequently affect teens. It trains them with appropriate actions to take in situations when a friend is struggling.

> **"I had noticed some signs in my friend I was concerned about, and I wouldn't have even thought about it if I hadn't taken the training."[45]**
>
> —Oliver Hernandez-Norris, high school student who took a Mental Health First Aid course

Ottumwa High School in New Jersey was one of the first schools to implement the course for its students. In 2023 then tenth grader Oliver Hernandez-Norris underwent the course and soon used it to assist a friend. "I had noticed some signs in my friend I was concerned about, and I wouldn't have even thought about it if I hadn't taken the training,"[45] he says. His friend was withdrawn, not participating in normal activities, and

Peer mental health support benefits not only those struggling but also those providing the help.

demonstrating anger. Hernandez-Norris says the training helped him see that these were potential signs of depression. He messaged the school counselor, who also leads the program. She talked to him about what to say to his friend, and then he called his friend. After talking with the friend and asking the friend to hang out, Herandez-Norris determined he was not in a crisis but was going through a tough time. Being there for his friend was what the friend needed.

Benefits to Self

Peer mental health support benefits not only those struggling but also those providing the help. For many, being there for others dealing with mental health issues allows them to understand and empathize more easily with people. It also teaches them to be more aware of others as an active observer and listener.

Teens have also found that the training they undergo benefits their own mental health. Von Conley found this to be the case after taking the peer mental health support training at Ottumwa High School in 2023. "When we went over all the warning signs of someone who was like, spiraling, I recognized a lot of those behaviors in myself," Conley says. "When I'm not feeling great, I tend to withdraw from everyone. In the moment I felt like I needed to do something better for myself—I needed to confide in the people I love instead of hiding it."[46] The training gave Conley the courage to do just that.

In addressing the mental health challenges teens face today, teen-to-teen programs and initiatives provide more than just crisis intervention—they develop a supportive community where teens feel heard, understood, and empowered to help one another. By teaching vital mental health skills and developing emotional awareness, peer programs benefit both those receiving help and those offering it. Teens, equipped with the right tools, can be instrumental in promoting mental well-being and preventing crises in their communities.

Introduction: Teens Can Have an Impact

1. Quoted in Robert S. Wolf, "Metairie Teen Designs an App Offering Music, Meditation and More to Improve Mental Health," Nola, September 23, 2023. www.nola.com.
2. Quoted in Wolf, "Metairie Teen Designs an App Offering Music, Meditation and More to Improve Mental Health."
3. Quoted in Share Care, "How Sports Education Creates Empathy of Children with Special Needs," 2023. www.sharecare.com.
4. Quoted in Share Care, "How Sports Education Creates Empathy of Children with Special Needs."
5. Quoted in Wolf, "Metairie Teen Designs an App Offering Music, Meditation and More to Improve Mental Health."

Chapter One: Many Needs, Many Benefits

6. Quoted in Carolyn Jones, "Peer Counseling Gains Popularity as California Schools Beef Up Student Mental Health," Ed Source, February 18, 2022. https://edsource.org.
7. Quoted in Medium, "Unstoppable: How Chrissy Has Redefined Success While Navigating Society with Teen Depression," September 9, 2024. https://medium.com.
8. Quoted in Jones, "Peer Counseling Gains Popularity as California Schools Beef Up Student Mental Health."
9. Quoted in Laura Newberry, "Amid a Youth Mental Health Crisis, Teens Help One Another," *Los Angeles Times*, December 20, 2021. www.latimes.com.
10. Quoted in Carolyn Twersky, "Thandiwe Abdullah Is Leading the Next Generation of the Black Lives Matter Movement," *Seventeen*, December 1, 2020. www.seventeen.com.
11. Quoted in Jones, "Peer Counseling Gains Popularity as California Schools Beef Up Student Mental Health."
12. Quoted in Savio Clemente, "Sadie Keller: I Survived Cancer and Here Is How I Did It," Medium, November 14, 2021. https://medium.com.
13. Quoted in Kerry Kulkarni, "Miss Amazing Grows Confidence and Self-Esteem in Watertown Woman with Disabilities," *Watertown (SD) Public Opinion*, February 21, 2022. www.thepublicopinion.com.

Chapter Two: Teens Supporting Bullied Peers

14. Ryan Walker, "I'm a Teenager Who Was Bullied: Here's What Bullying Among Teens Looks like Today," *Parents*, June 29, 2022. www.parents.com.
15. Walker, "I'm a Teenager Who Was Bullied."
16. Walker, "I'm a Teenager Who Was Bullied."
17. Darby Fox, "A New Approach to Stop Bullying," *Rethinking Your Teenager* (blog), *Psychology Today*, April 20, 2024. www.psychologytoday.com.
18. Quoted in Mike Vulpo, "Meet 15 Kids Who Prove You're Never Too Young to Change the World," E! Online, September 5, 2021. www.eonline.com.
19. Quoted in Project Rockit, "Be the Solution, Call Out Harmful Behavior, the Reward Is Greater than the Risk," Facebook, September 3, 2024. www.facebook.com.
20. Jay Taylor, "Believing in Better Is Critical for LGBTQ+ Youth Survival!" It Gets Better, December 19, 2023. https://itgetsbetter.org.
21. Jamie, "About Jamie," Pacer Center's Teens Against Bullying, 2024. www.pacerteensagainstbullying.org.
22. Jamie, "Jamie's Advice," Pacer Center's Teens Against Bullying, 2024. www.pacerteensagainstbullying.org.

Chapter Three: Teens Tutoring Teens

23. Quoted in Schoolhouse.world, "Schoolhouse Stories." https://schoolhouse.world.
24. Ava Hazzouri, "The Value of Getting—and Giving—Peer Tutoring," PBS, August 6, 2021. www.pbs.org.
25. Quoted in University of Idaho, "Both Mayda and Ashley Got the Pleasure of Watching Mayda's Algebra Grade Improve." www.webpages.uidaho.edu.
26. Hazzouri, "The Value of Getting—and Giving—Peer Tutoring."
27. Quoted in Schoolhouse.world, "Schoolhouse Stories."
28. Hazzouri, "The Value of Getting—and Giving—Peer Tutoring."
29. Quoted in Hazzouri, "The Value of Getting—and Giving—Peer Tutoring."
30. Quoted in Schoolhouse.world, "Schoolhouse Stories."
31. Quoted in Boone County Schools, *Peer Tutoring at Ockerman Middle School*, YouTube, 2024. www.youtube.com/watch?v=OHn9O8fDyB0.

Chapter Four: Teen Mentors

32. Quoted in University of Bristol, *3 Things to Know About Peer Mentoring*, YouTube, 2021. www.youtube.com/watch?v=SWV9umtq4co.
33. Quoted in Jacob Phillips, "Peer-Mentoring Program Helping First-Year UVA Students," 29 News, August 27, 2023. www.29news.com.
34. Quoted in Stacey Eidson, "Making Lifelong Connections with the Jags4Jags Mentoring Program at Augusta University," JagWire, February 14, 2024. https://jagwire.augusta.edu.
35. Quoted in Eidson, "Making Lifelong Connections with the Jags4-Jags Mentoring Program at Augusta University."
36. Quoted in Laura Hutchinson, "What's Right with Schools: Upperclassmen Lend a Helping Hand to Freshmen," News 8, October 8, 2024. www.wtnh.com.
37. Quoted in Hutchinson, "What's Right with Schools."
38. Quoted in Oak Foundation, "Eye to Eye—Mentoring Children at Schools Across the United States," August 5, 2021. https://oakfnd.org.
39. Quoted in Amanda Beeler, "Eye to Eye: Creating Supportive Communities for PA Students with Learning Disabilities," International Dyslexia Association Pennsylvania, March 10, 2023. https://pa.dyslexiaida.org.

Chapter Five: Mental Health Help

40. Quoted in Peter Medlin, "Crystal Lake Schools Expand Mental Health Services, Including Free Teletherapy," Hope Squad, October 8, 2024. https://hopesquad.com.
41. Mental Health America, "Youth Peer Support," 2024. www.mhanational.org.
42. Quoted in "Tara's Experience Opening Up To a Friend About Depression," Reach Out, September 5, 2023. https://au.reachout.com.
43. Quoted in Meredith Moran, "Student-Led Hope Squads Give Students a Peer to Talk To," Hope Squad, June 12, 2024. https://hopesquad.com.
44. Aidan, "Brighter Days," National Institute on Minority Health and Health Disparities, September 20, 2022. www.nimhd.nih.gov.
45. Quoted in Anya Kamenetz, "A Surprising Remedy for Teens in Mental Health Crises," Hechinger Report, March 3, 2023. https://hechingerreport.org.
46. Quoted in Kamenetz, "A Surprising Remedy for Teens in Mental Health Crises."

FOR FURTHER RESEARCH

Books

Heidi Crow, *Teen Mental Health; A Guide to Understanding and Supporting Teen Mental Health: Today's Teenagers; Navigating Mental Health in a Digital World*. Self-published, 2024.

Sameer Hinduja, *Bullying Beyond the Schoolyard: Preventing and Responding to Cyberbullying*. Thousand Oaks, CA: Corwin, 2023.

Daniel Sanford, *The Rowman & Littlefield Guide for Peer Tutors*. Lanham, MD: Rowman & Littlefield, 2020.

Stan Wilson, *Teen Leadership Unlocked: Teen's Empowerment Essentials: Unlocking the Secrets to Effective Leadership*. Self-published, 2024.

Internet Sources

Annie E. Casey Foundation, "Spotlight on Youth Mentoring," January 24, 2024. www.aecf.org.

Meg Dunn, "This Unique Mentorship Program Helps Students with Learning Differences Realize 'Their Brains Are Beautiful,'" CNN, March 18, 2021. www.cnn.com.

Mara Klecker, "At One Woodbury School, Teens Saw the Achievement Gap and Stepped Up to Tutor Their Peers," *Minneapolis (MN) Star Tribune*, November 7, 2023. www.startribune.com.

Maria Lockwood, "Superior High School Peers Connect in Nature to Prevent Suicides," *Duluth (MN) Superior Telegram*, October 14, 2024. www.superiortelegram.com.

Mental Health First Aid, "10 Ways to Help Someone Who Is Struggling with Their Mental Health," October 14, 2024. www.mentalhealthfirstaid.org.

Tiffany Millacci, "Anti-bullying Programs in Schools: 23+ Best Activities," Positive Psychology, June 25, 2022. https://positivepsychology.com.

National Mentoring Resource Center, "Peer Mentoring," 2024. https://nationalmentoringresourcecenter.org.

Websites

Hope Squad

https://hopesquad.com

Hope Squad is a peer-to-peer mental health support program that trains students to recognize the signs of distress in their classmates. By equipping teens with the skills to intervene early, Hope Squad empowers students to take action in times of crisis. Its website offers tools for mental health awareness and suicide prevention.

Neurodiversity Disability Alliance (NDA)

https://thendalliance.org

Eye to Eye is a key mentorship program of NDA that pairs middle and high school students with learning differences or ADHD with trained college or high school mentors who share similar challenges. The website provides information on this program and how to get involved.

988 Suicide & Crisis Lifeline

https://988lifeline.org

The 988 Suicide & Crisis Lifeline is a national network of crisis centers that provides support to people in crisis. It operates twenty-four hours a day, seven days a week. Its website provides information on suicide prevention, risk factors and symptoms, and stories of hope and recovery. If you or someone you know is experiencing emotional distress or thoughts of suicide, call 988 for help.

PACER's National Bullying Prevention Center

https://pacer.org/bullying

PACER's National Bullying Prevention Center offers tools for teens to actively combat bullying in their schools and communities. The website features resources for starting anti-bullying initiatives, as well as educational materials on the harmful effects of bullying.

Schoolhouse.world

https://schoolhouse.world

Schoolhouse.world is a free online platform that connects students with peer tutors in a wide variety of subjects. By providing online peer-to-peer tutoring, the platform helps students of all ages improve academically through individualized sessions. This site also provides information on the process and training to become a peer tutor.

StopBullying.gov

https://stopbullying.gov

StopBullying.gov is a resource from the US government aimed at preventing bullying among youth. The site provides guidance on how teens, parents, and educators can recognize, address, and prevent bullying behaviors. It offers strategies for creating safer school environments and promoting positive behavior in peer interactions.

Note: Boldface page numbers indicate illustrations.

Abdullah, Thandiwe, 13
academics
  college/university peer mentoring programs, 36–40, **37**
  English language learning, 31
  high school peer mentoring programs, 40–41
  percentage of students struggling with, 27–28
  See also peer tutoring
academic success, peer mentoring and, 41
active listening, 49
Adirondack Lilly, 15
AIM Academy (Pennsylvania), 42–43
AIMS College Prep Middle School (California), 31
American Academy of Pediatrics, 46
Amity Regional High School (Woodbridge, Connecticut), 40–41
anxiety and bullying, 10
arts, building self-esteem through, 20, 21
Augusta University (Georgia), 38

Baker, Justin, 50
Banihashemi, Adria, 31
belonging, sense of, 16
Bennett, Gracyn, 38–40
Black Lives Matter (BLM) movement, 13
Black youth, 46
Blue Ribbon Week, 25
Buanga, Kevin, 34–35
bullying
  breaking cycle of
    anti-bullying marches, 25
    intervention and, 26
    programs to teach bystander intervention, 21–23, **22**
    reporting, to persons in charge, 18
    using arts to empower victims, 20, 21
  of LGBTQ youth, 21
  percentage of teenagers experiencing, 10
  on social media, 17–19, **18**
  stigma of being victim of, 26
  strategies to support victims of, 21–23, **22**
  suicide and, 10, 21, 25
Bureau of Justice Statistics, 10

cancer, helping children with, 15
Cardona, Ashley, 29, 30
Carson, Susan, 43
Center for Education Policy Research, 28
Centers for Disease Control and Prevention, 45, 46
Certner, Matthew, 5–6
Chadbourne, Sadie, 40
communication skills
  building, by helping others, 7, 14, 38
  importance of listening, 8
compassion and empathy, building, by helping others, 7, 35, 38
confidence. *See* self-esteem

Congressional App Challenge, 5
Conley, Von, 52
Cool 2 Be Kind, 25
COVID-19 pandemic, 45
C.S. Mott Children's Hospital National Poll on Children's Health, 11
Cuellar, Alina, 41
cyberbullying, 17–19, **18**, 21

depression, percentage of teenagers with episodes of, 10
disabilities, teenagers with. *See* special needs, teenagers with
Donovan, Gabriel, 15

eating disorders, treatment centers for teenagers with, 7
Education Endowment Foundation, 33
empathy and compassion, building, by helping others, 7, 35, 38
empowerment
  gaining, by helping others, 13
  using social media through experiences of celebrities, 23–24
Eye to Eye, 42, 43

Ferretti, Millie, 49
Flink, David, 42
Fox, Darby, 19
Free2Luv, 20, 21

gender and cyberbullying, 21
gender and mental well-being, 46
Gonzalez, Christopher, 8–9
Graham, Jennifer, 41
Green, Miah, 19–20
gun violence, 11

Hazzouri, Ava, 28–29, 30, 33
helpers, benefits to, 7, 14, 38
  developing compassion, 35
  developing leadership abilities, 35
  empowerment, 13
  increase in self-esteem of, 7, 13, 32, 33
  own mental health, 52
  sense of fulfillment, 33–34
Hernandez-Norris, Oliver, 51–52
high school peer mentoring programs, 40–41
Hispanic youth, 46
Hope Squad, 44, 48–49

It Gets Better (video), 23
It Gets Better organization, 23–24

Jags4Jags program, 39–40
Jones, Skylar, 16
Journal of Adolescence, 13

Keller, Sadie, 15
Kumbala, Vaishnavi, 4–5, 7

Lambert, Adam, 23–24, **24**
leadership abilities, building, by helping others, 13–14, 35, 38
Lexley, Angel, 39–40
LGBTQ youth
  bullying of, 21
  mental health challenges and, 45–46
  percentage of, considering suicide, 14, 21
  Trevor Project and, 14
Lily Pads, 43
Link Crew, 38, 40–41
listening, importance of, 8

Mann, Michael, 32–33
March for Our Lives, 11
Marjory Stoneman Douglas High School (Parkland, Florida), 11
McPherson, Baylee, 11–12, 14
Mental Health America, 47

mental well-being
app to improve, 4–5
benefits to counselors', 52
common mental health issues, 44–45, **45**, 47
COVID-19 pandemic and, 45
gender and, 46
of LGBTQ youth, 45–46
peer mentor programs supporting, 44, 48–50
signs of needing immediate help, 50
of teenagers of color, 46
See also peer counseling
Miss Amazing organization, 16
Muravnik, Matthew, 41
Murillo, Mayda, 29, 30

National Center for Education Statistics, 10, 27
National Council for Mental Wellbeing, 50
National Institute of Mental Health, 10, 44–45

Ottumwa High School (New Jersey), 51–52

PACER's National Bullying Prevention Center, 21–22
peer counseling
accessibility of, 12, **12**
benefits to mental well-being of counselors, 52
maintaining healthy boundaries and, 46
mental well-being and, 8
parents' support for, 11
teenagers' ability to speak to and understand each other and, 11–12, 13, 47–48, **48**, 49
training programs, 44, 48–51
youth-led anti-bullying workshops, 22–23
peer mentoring
academic success and, 41
at colleges and universities, 36–40, **37**
at high schools, 40–41
for mental health support, 44, 48–50
personal connections created by, 38–40, **39**
for teenagers with special needs, 42–43, **43**
training programs, 38
peer tutoring, **28**
benefits of, 32–33
cross-cultural friendships developing from, 31
examples of, 27, 28–29
group, 30
online, 27, 30–31, **32**
reasons for success of, 29–30
training for, 34
Perez, Angeles, 12–13
Peterson, Ava, 44, 45
Pew Research Center, 10, 19, 21
problem-solving abilities, building, by helping others, 14
Project HEAL, 7
Project Rockit, 22–23

Rosenman, Liana, 6–7

Sadie Keller Foundation, 15
Saffran, Kristina, 6–7
San Clemente High School (California), 25
Saplings (app), 4–5
Schoolhouse.world
ease of using, 31
SAT tutoring, 33
success with, 27

training to become peer tutors for, 34
self-esteem
building
by helping others, 7, 13, 32, 33
of teenagers with disabilities, 16
through arts, 20, 21
bullying and, 10, 25–26
Silverman, Morgan, 43
social media
bullying on
breaking cycle of, 18, 19–20, 21–23, **22**
described, 17, **18**
experiences, 20
negative effects of, 10
peer tutoring on, 27, 30–31, **32**
using, to empower teenagers, 23–24
Somer, Jordan, 15–16
Sparks, Kyia, 38
special needs, teenagers with
athletic activities centers for, 5–6
beauty pageants for, 15–16
peer mentoring and, 42–43, **43**
technology to empower, 15
Special Needs Athletic Program, 6
sports centers for teenagers with disabilities, 5–6
Stanford Open Policing Project, 46
Study Hard Project, 28–29, 33
Stutzman, Becky, 5
suicide
bullying and, 10, 25
gender and, 21
percentage of LGBTQ teenagers considering, 14, 21, 46
signs individual needs immediate help, 50
Suicide & Crisis Lifeline, 50

Taylor, Jay, 23, 24
teamwork abilities, building, by helping others, 13–14
teenagers of color, mental well-being of, 46
Teen Lifeline, 49–50
Teen Mental Health First Aid, 50–51
Teens Against Bullying (website), 26
Trevor Project, 14, 21, 46
Tyler Clementi Foundation, 18

University of Bristol, 36
University of Virginia (UVA), 37

Wald, Cassidy, 42
Walker, Ryan, 17–18, 19
wellness checks, 44
Western Governors University, 41
White, Maddie, 43

Youth Risk Behavior Survey (2023, Centers for Disease Control and Prevention), 45

Cover: Gorgev/Shutterstock

6: Monkey Business Images/Shutterstock
9: Ground Picture/Shutterstock
12: Monkey Business Images/Shutterstock
18: PeopleImages.com - Yuri A/Shutterstock
22: Daniel Hoz/Shutterstock
24: Debby Wong/Shutterstock
28: BongkarnGraphic/Shutterstock
32: Prostock-studio/Shutterstock
37: PeopleImages.com - Yuri A/Shutterstock
39: Giulio_Fornasar/Shutterstock
43: Ollyy/Shutterstock
45: Motortion Films/Shutterstock
48: Monkey Business Images/Shutterstock
51: ersaguncelebi/Shutterstock

Leanne Currie-McGhee has written books for the past two decades. She lives in Norfolk, Virginia, with her husband, Keith, daughters, Grace and Sol, and their dog, Delilah.